Indoor Sports

Lucy Simonds

Contents

Inside, not out	2
Knock them down	4
In the pocket	6
In the net	8
On court	10
Anyone for tennis?	12
Hit the target	14
Sum up	16

OXFORD
UNIVERSITY PRESS

Inside, not out

Many sports are played inside. Why?

How many sports on these 2 pages use a ball?

KEY WORDS

- how many?
- more than
- count
- count on

This book looks at 9 ball sports. Can you find them? How many are not shown on these two pages?

Find how many more people are playing table tennis than bowling.

TOOLS

| 1 | 2 | 3 | 4 | 5 | 6 | 7 | 8 | 9 | 10 |

Knock them down

In tenpin bowling the players roll a ball down the lane to knock down pins.

There are 10 pins in total. How many are hidden?

How many pins have been knocked down?

Skittles is like tenpin bowling but there are fewer skittles than pins to knock down.

KEY WORDS
- count
- how many?
- left
- fewer

5 skittles are knocked down. How many are left standing?

Jack knocks down all the pins and all the skittles. How many are knocked down?

TOOLS

In the pocket

In snooker, players knock the coloured balls into pockets with the white ball.

There are 15 red balls at the start of every game. How many have been potted?

FACT! The highest score from potting all the balls is 147 points.

- 1 point
- 2 points
- 3 points
- 4 points
- 5 points
- 6 points
- 7 points

Why do players want to pot the black? Find a colour worth 3 points less than the black.

KEY WORDS
- how many?
- how many more?
- less
- count on

Pool is like snooker but fewer balls are used. Players pot balls with spots or stripes.

How many more balls are used in snooker than in pool?

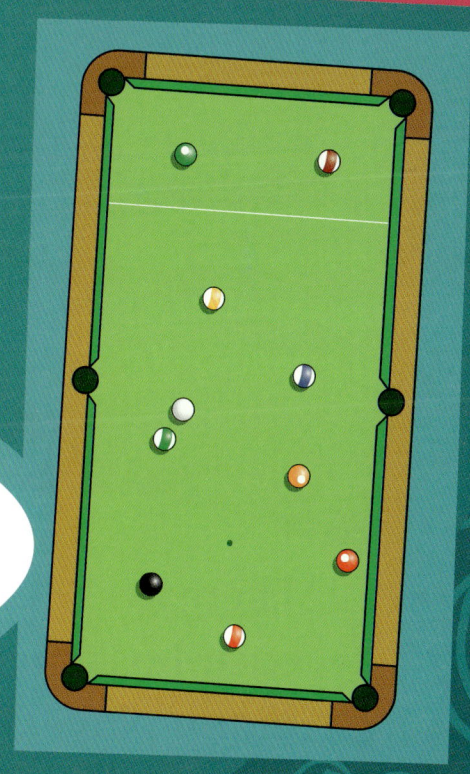

The black ball does not count as a spot. Who is winning, spots or stripes?

TOOLS

| 1 | 2 | 3 | 4 | 5 | 6 | 7 | 8 | 9 | 10 |
| 11 | 12 | 13 | 14 | 15 | 16 | 17 | 18 | 19 | 20 |

In the net

Basketball is usually played on an indoor court.

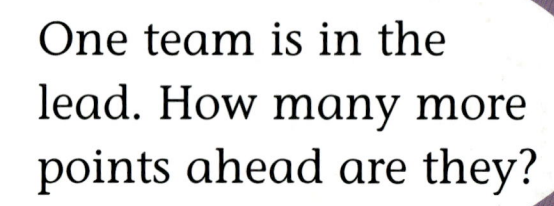

HOME VISITOR
8   12

One team is in the lead. How many more points ahead are they?

FACT! 60 thousand people is the record for a crowd at a basketball game.

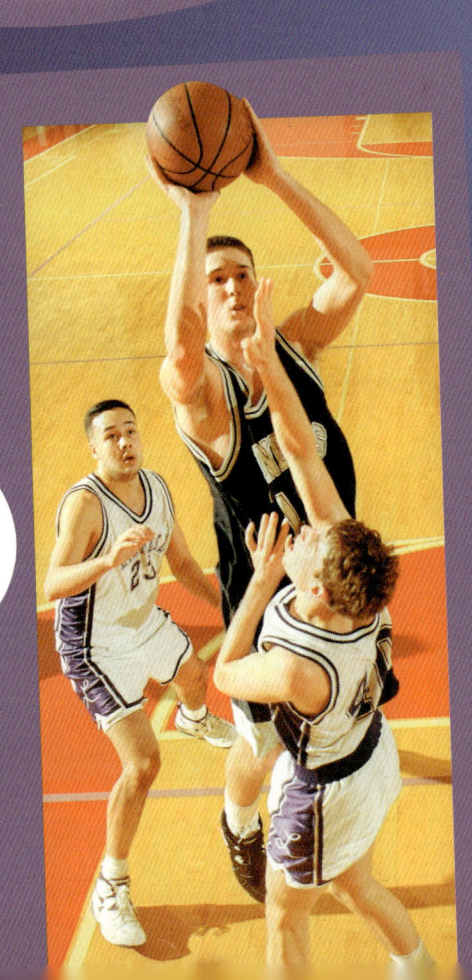

There are 5 players in each basketball team. How many players are missing from the picture?

KEY WORDS

- fewer
- count
- how many more?

Indoor football teams have fewer players than outdoor teams. Count the players on each team.

How many more players are in an outdoor football team?

If players change from playing outside to inside, how many cannot play?

TOOLS

1	2	3	4	5	6	7	8	9	10
11	12	13	14	15	16	17	18	19	20
21	22	23	24	25	26	27	28	29	30

On court

Badminton players hit a shuttlecock over a high net. They try to stop it landing on the floor.

The first team to reach 15 points wins. The score is 12–7. How many points does each team need to win?

KEY WORDS

- more
- how many?
- count

Squash players score points by hitting the ball between the lines on a wall. The first to 9 points wins.

How many more points are needed in badminton than in squash?

Players have to beat the person whose name is above theirs. How many games must Rob win to reach the top?

Harry
Sanjay
Michael
Dylan
Rob
Raj
John
Alex
Dev
James

TOOLS

| 1 | 2 | 3 | 4 | 5 | 6 | 7 | 8 | 9 | 10 |
| 11 | 12 | 13 | 14 | 15 | 16 | 17 | 18 | 19 | 20 |

Anyone for tennis?

Table tennis is played over a small net. The winner is the first to score 11 points.

Who is in the lead in each game?

FACT!

At the World Championships more than 700 players compete from more than 130 countries.

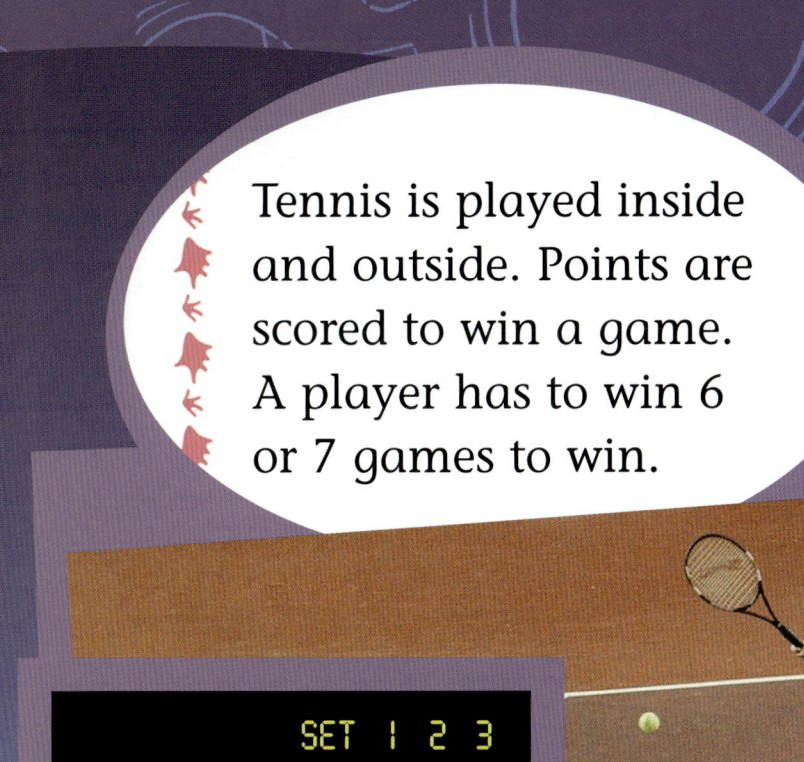

KEY WORDS

- difference
- count on
- first
- how many more?

Tennis is played inside and outside. Points are scored to win a game. A player has to win 6 or 7 games to win.

SET	1	2	3
HENMAN	7	3	4
RODDICK*	5	6	2

Find the difference between the number of games won by each player in each set.

Who has won the most games in the match?

TOOLS

1	2	3	4	5	6	7	8	9	10
11	12	13	14	15	16	17	18	19	20

Hit the target

In darts, players take turns to throw three darts at the board. They take away the score from the starting number. The first person to reach 0 is the winner.

FACT! It takes only 9 throws to reach 0 from 501... if you hit the right numbers!

yellow	red
~~20~~	~~25~~
~~18~~	~~17~~
12	15

Which dart has scored the most?

Count back to find each team's new score.

Dan started with 20. He hit 3, 7 and 6 with his 3 darts. How much is left?

14

In archery, arrows are shot at a target. Which target has the highest score? How much less is the lowest score?

KEY WORDS
- total
- take away
- left
- how much less?

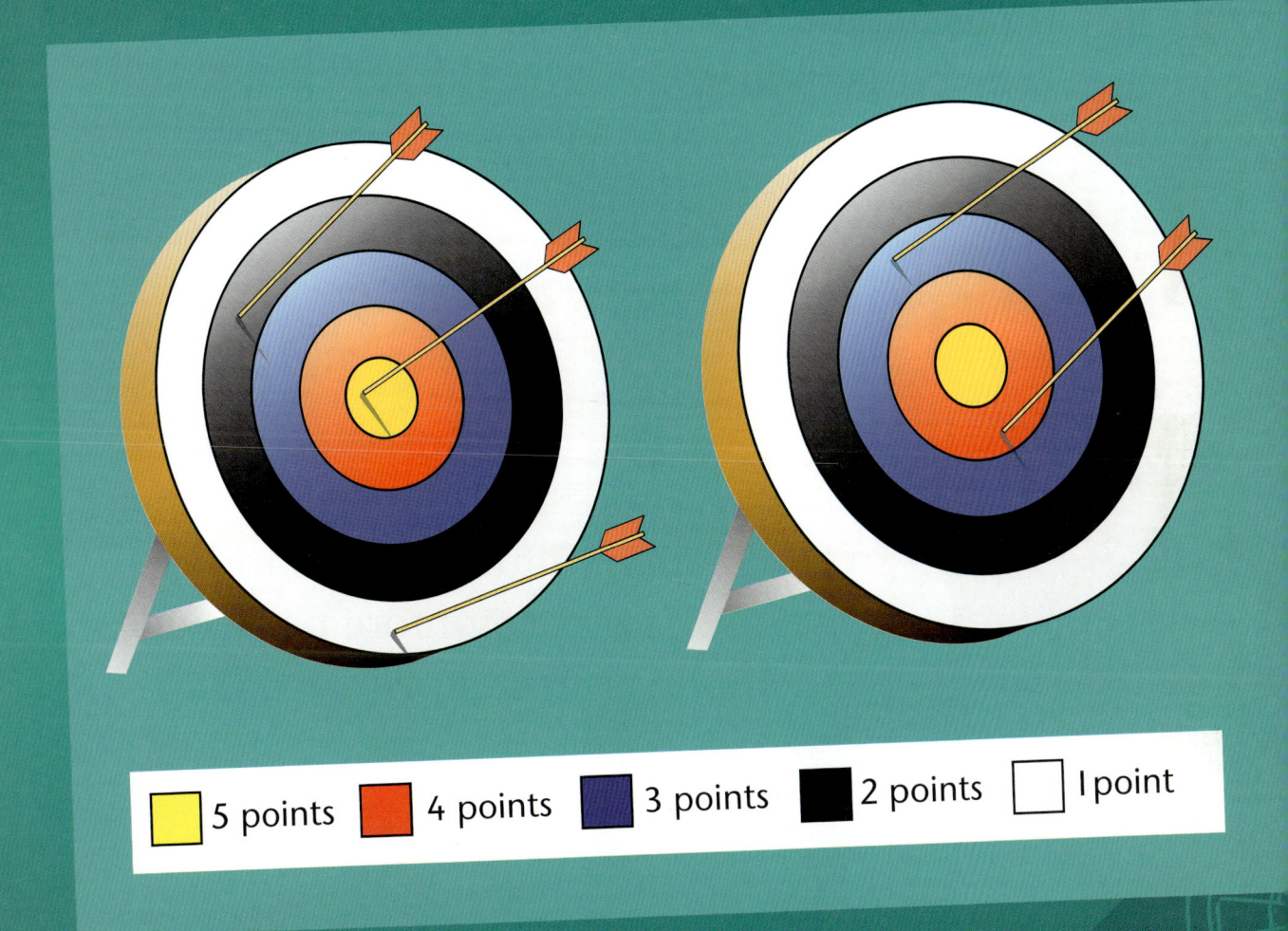

- 5 points
- 4 points
- 3 points
- 2 points
- 1 point

TOOLS

| 1 | 2 | 3 | 4 | 5 | 6 | 7 | 8 | 9 | 10 |
| 11 | 12 | 13 | 14 | 15 | 16 | 17 | 18 | 19 | 20 |

15

Sum up

There are 11 players in an outdoor football team, 5 of them also belong to a basketball team. How many do not play basketball?

The score in a table tennis match is 6–4. How many more points does each player need to win?

In a basketball match one team has 15 points, the other has 8. What is the difference in their scores?